THE ART OF

Driftwood AND

Dried Arrangements

THE ART OF *Driftwood* AND

BY TATSUO ISHIMOTO

author of THE ART OF FLOWER ARRANGEMENT

Dried Arrangements

AVENEL BOOKS

New York

The author is indebted to many people and groups for assistance in preparation of this book. Particular thanks are due the following:

DRIFTWOOD:	Desert Treasures Palm Spring, California
	Driftin's Inc. Portland, Oregon
	Hoseabo Gig Harbor, Washington
CONTAINERS:	Gray-N-Ware San Francisco, California
	T. Z. Shiota San Francisco, California
WEEDS:	Floral Service San Mateo, California
FIGURES:	New China Import and Export San Francisco, California

This book is dedicated to the following
good friends whose help and advice helped make it possible:

PAUL ANDERSON • DAVID BOTSFORD JR. • LUCILLE EDGREN
AZZIE AND ELDRED IRELAND • CLIFFORD HICKOX • BETTY FARIS
THOMAS KING • ESTHER AND JACK MELLQUIST • JAMES DAVY

Table of Contents

Foreword

Most adult Americans have recognized the need for and have acquired a hobby. Many have several. They collect antiques, grow flowers, save stamps, build furniture, make photographs, hook rugs, do all sorts of sane and zany things.

It so happens that I like flowers and I enjoy arranging them. Also, I am a photographer, and I get a special satisfaction from working with lighting and abstract compositions.

Ever since I did *The Art of Flower Arrangement* I have wanted to develop a similar, simple approach to driftwood and dried arrangements—the next logical step in the direction of abstract composition for any enthusiastic flower arranger.

The popularity of driftwood arrangements has been growing at an astonishing rate in the past few years. And little wonder. What a challenge there is for the flower arranger when she first turns to driftwood. Here is material that lends itself to the utmost subtlety of treatment. Here shapes and textures are not overwhelmed by the competing color of flowers. Here are the bare bones of nature herself—wood, stones, branches, weathered by wind, sun, and water.

Here is fresh enjoyment and endless opportunity for anyone who enjoys flower arrangement—for anyone, in fact, who enjoys nature and natural materials.

————

This book has been three years in the making. In that time I have collected a studio full of driftwood pieces. Many of them, by now, are old friends—handled and used in countless ways, countless times. Photographs have piled up by the hundreds. The editing and final selection have not been easy, but many friendly critics have helped in making the choices published here.

T.I.

San Francisco, California

What goes into a dry arrangement?

Almost anything you want to put into it. I like to create three-dimensional pictures—half abstract, half real, pictures which suggest something fresh and different each time I look at them.

That's one reason that I like to use figurines in my arrangements. I see in a piece of driftwood the look of a rocky granite cliff. I mount it so—perpendicular and towering. Then I put at the base a few stones—they help suggest the rocky nature of my cliff. A leafless branch towers over my driftwood—it is a tree. Last, I put in my figurine. A third the height of the driftwood piece, it establishes scale. Here is a cliff that towers over a man. Others disagree on figurines. No people, they say. No dogs, no ducks, no Chinese patriarchs. Let the arrangement use natural materials only. Let it remain an abstract composition. Let the imagination fill in the details.

That point of view is quite all right with me. Every arranger to his or her own taste. You are the one to be pleased.

If you do adopt my view, remember this when you buy figurines to use with arrangements: select those with movement or a natural pose. For example, modern wood sculpture provides many excellent figures with clean, simple lines.

You don't have to live on the coast of California or Maine to start a driftwood collection.

What is driftwood, really? It is simply wood which has weathered. Its shape and texture and color may easily be the work of wind action, not wave action; of fresh water, not salt water; of sun-bleaching and sun-drying in Nebraska or Wisconsin, not in Florida or Oregon.

Where do you find driftwood? It's just a matter of looking for it. If you live on either coast you are lucky, of course. Walk the beach and you'll find wonderful pieces ready and waiting for you. After a time you'll develop a special eye for driftwood. In their lines and textures, pieces will suggest a stone outcropping or a miniature mountain range, a softly rounded hillside or a sharply edged cliff. Other pieces will delight your eye as almost wholly abstract, yet natural, forms.

Can you make similar discoveries away from the coast? Of course you can. Go for walks in the country—driftwood explorations. Look at the edges of ploughed fields with woodlots close by. Look along lake shores. Look along stream beds, especially on gravel bars in summer when the water is low. Look in the woods. Some of the finest driftwood finds are made in Minnesota-lake country, not ocean country. Beautiful pieces turn up in the Connecticut hills.

If you are an inlander and want to add some authentic seacoast driftwood to your collection, you can buy pieces by mail. Several reliable firms, ranging in location from Puget Sound in Washington State to Southern California, collect and sell driftwood. A number of the pieces used in the arrangements in this book were bought by mail from such collectors.

Another wonderful source of weathered wood is the American desert. Collectors love to prowl the desert areas of Nevada, Southern Utah, Arizona, and New Mexico, and especially the Mojave, Colorado, and Borrego deserts in California. This desert driftwood is also for sale—several firms will send pieces by mail.

In the texts accompanying the arrangements, I have listed the sources of a few of the driftwood pieces. There was no point listing all since I gathered practically my entire collection on the West Coast.

How about equipment?

What do you need in the way of equipment to make dry arrangements? Very little, indeed. If you are a flower arranger, you probably own several shallow containers. You are familiar with needle holders and you use modeling clay to secure these holders to the floor of the container.

If you are new at arranging, don't worry about these details. Most florists stock both needle holders and clay. Get yourself several holders, in a variety of shapes and sizes. They are not very expensive, and you'll find use for every one you buy.

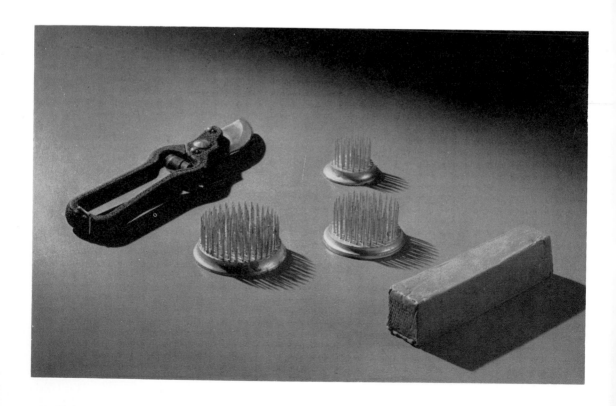

Containers are another matter

The best container for a dry arrangement, in my view, isn't a container at all. There is no water to contain, so why bother with walls that will conceal the base of your dry arrangement?

What you really want is a base or platform. Many things will serve as such a base. An almost flat wooden tray will do. So will some modern pottery platters. A polished thin wood plank is better. Or you can make, or have made, some special bases of your own.

Here is what I use:

The bases are made of quarter-inch masonite. The material is cut in ovals, circles, rectangles, squares, free forms. Then it is painted. I use spray lacquer; friends of mine have had equally good success with brushed-on enamel. They have used plywood as well as masonite.

Some friends have tried colors on their arrangement platforms. All of mine are spray-painted in black, various values of gray, or off-white. But I must admit that a pale yellow, a blue, or a crimson base sometimes makes a very interesting contrast to the gray values present in most dry arrangements.

You can, of course, also use shallow pottery containers for your dry compositions. If you do, pick those with the lowest possible sides. Avoid bright shades, avoid almost all patterns or figures, use only plain, neutral shades.

How can you make your driftwood stand up?

There are many ways to fix your driftwood pieces securely to your container. Often all you need to do is punch the wood firmly into a needle holder, and then fix the holder to the container with clay. If the clay doesn't give enough support, use rocks or stones for additional bracing.

Sometimes stones alone are all you need to stand your driftwood firmly in place.

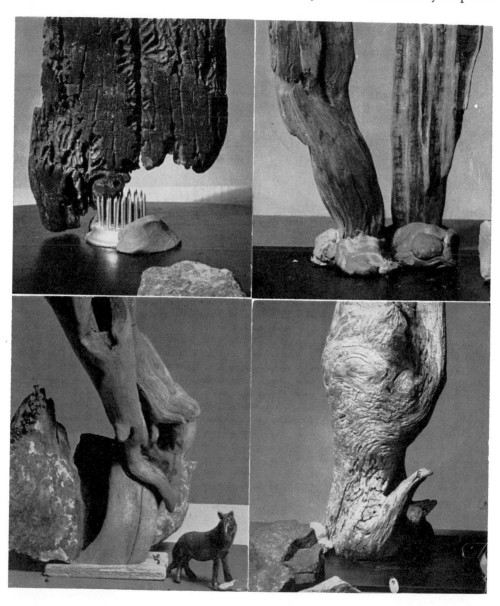

Sometimes stones, plus a little clay, will do the job. Often the wood piece will stand by itself.

I have altered some of my driftwood pieces slightly to make them easier to use in arrangements. I have nailed a small, flat wood base on some large curved pieces. I have trimmed one end of several pieces with a saw.

This is the way I usually start to arrange:

First I decide where I want to place the arrangement. Obviously this will affect what I do with my material. If it is to go on a low coffee table where it will be seen from above, the arrangement will be quite different from one placed higher, on a radio, a bookcase or a mantel. If it is to be placed against a wall I have to consider how it will appear from one side, while an arrangement placed, for example, on a table in the center of a room must look well from all sides.

Next I determine the size and color of the arrangement. Seldom will color be a problem, since the prevailing grays and browns of driftwood, rocks and dry weeds are quite neutral and blend happily in any surroundings. The size of the completed arrangement, however, is important. It should "fit." By this I mean simply that a large arrangement on a small table in most circumstances will seem out of place; it will appear to overpower the table. Similarly, a small arrangement on a very large table will be lost.

Think of your arrangement as a part of your whole decorative scheme. Its proportions, like those of your chairs, tables and draperies, should be in harmony with its surroundings.

Next I decide what will be the main object of my arrangement, and what secondary materials I will use. A piece of wood, a rock, a group of weeds, a figure—one of these will dominate the arrangement.

Then I must determine how to hold my main object in place. If it is a piece of wood, perhaps I will use a needle holder, clay or rocks to hold it erect. Or perhaps I will have to saw off one end of the wood.

Weeds and other secondary material probably can be held in place with a needle holder and clay.

The final result is a combination of the materials I have used and the thought I have given to them. If the result pleases me—good. If I am dissatisfied, I change it.

Here are four simple rules which may prove helpful:

1. Be sure that the size and color of your main object and container will fit harmoniously in the location you have chosen for your arrangement.

2. Keep the arrangement simple, with one object standing out more than the others.

3. Use different heights and different amounts of materials. Try to avoid placing two objects of the same height or size in the same arrangement.

4. If possible, add an accent. This can be a small piece of odd material, a figure, a bit of bright color. Just a touch of contrast can add a great deal to an arrangement that otherwise might appear dull or ordinary.

When you have selected the main piece of driftwood, study it. Examine it from above, from below and from both sides. A little time devoted to such a study will be repaid many times over in the final arrangement.

Odd numbers are better than even numbers for good composition. The "rule of three" suggests the use of three objects of varying size.

Repetition of forms and shapes make for effective arrangements.

Add a small figure to make the main object appear larger.

Most important—turn your imagination loose: give your group a plot. This will provide the originality that produces the best arrangements.

A few simple rules to remember:

The mat or base should be proportionate to the size of your main object. This mat is too large. It makes the wood appear small.

The size of the mat is right. It appears to support the wood, gives it an adequate base while allowing the wood to remain the dominant center of interest.

All wrong. There is no one main object, since the weeds are the same height and seem to have the same mass as the wood. The needle holder is exposed to view.

All right. The wood dominates the arrangement. Fewer and shorter weeds provide a variety in height. The rocks have been moved to offer a foundation and to screen the needle holder and other mechanical supports.

Wrong. When two objects of the same height are placed together in an arrangement, both lose interest and the result is flat and dull.

Right. The wood dominates the scene. Shorter weeds have replaced the cone, offering a difference in height and an interesting contrast in texture.

An arrangement with wood and three rocks

The mat or tray is the base on which you'll build your arrangement. It can have any shape you like provided it is flat or very low. This one is a circular piece of black masonite, fifteen-and-a-half inches in diameter. A piece of painted plywood would do just as well.

Here's all you need for this arrangement: Wood, three rocks of varying sizes, a needle holder, modeling clay and the mat.

Use the needle holder and clay to hold your wood firmly in position.

This simple 1—2—3—4 procedure can give you many effective arrangements.

Start with the tallest object, the wood, then place your next tallest object, the large rock. Then the medium-sized rock and finally the small rock to balance and complete the arrangement. Notice how the rocks in this descending order appear to broaden out at the bottom to form a base for the pinnacle of wood.

Change your arrangement by adding to it

One arrangement can be given endless variety by the simple process of addition. Above, a piece of wild mustard adds a delicate trace of height to the arrangement on the preceding page.

(*Opposite*) The whole feeling of the arrangement changes when you add a small Chinese figure. It brings movement to it, and a feeling of thoughtfulness.

This process of addition, of course, can be overdone. Much of your arrangement will be dictated by where you place it. If it seems too large or overcrowded, take something away. If its seems too bare or sparse, add to it.

These are easy

In each of these two arrangements, the main object is so distinctive in character that the balance of the material flows naturally from it.

(*Above*) The wood was an unusual find, an arranger's dream. It is just seven inches high. Modeling clay holds it firmly to the tray. Its proportions are accented by rocks at the base and the sprays of dried pods.

(*Opposite*) The twelve-inch figure is the main object here. An odd-shaped piece of weathered beach wood, smooth rocks and moss-covered forest wood add to the feeling of age.

Containers should harmonize with arrangements

Modern black plastic trays and bowls sometimes make very effective containers for arrangements. In every case your base should add something to—or at least not detract from—the effect you have planned. Consider what the use of an ornate or patterned tray would have done to either of these arrangements.

(*Above*) The twisted desert wood is so unique in form and texture that nothing should diminish its interest. Rocks give it a solid foundation; the oval-shaped tray carries out the line of motion.

(*Opposite*) Notice how the shape of the dish holds up the dark brown desert wood and the seated figure. The eucalyptus pods were sprayed white, but natural weed pods would have served the same purpose.

Start
at
the
bottom

Your container (or platform) should *harmonize* with the arrangement you place on it. This, certainly, is an essential first step. Notice on these pages how the four container-platforms — square, rectangular, circular, oval — are all in *comfortable* relationship with the arrangements they support.

Think of your mat or containers as the stage on which you'll set your scene. The shape may suggest your arrangement.

A low container

Use what you have

For your arrangement the best base will be low and simple, but any number of flat shapes will do very well. The main point to remember, again, is *harmony*. Have your container, no matter what its shape, in a comfortable relationship with the arrangement it supports. Notice how all the arrangements here seem to fit naturally the shape of the container-platforms below.

Irregular shape

.. or a free form

It goes over

The same piece of wood can have many different shapes, depending upon where you place it. Here it might suggest a prehistoric monster.

It goes under

Turn him upside down, and your monster becomes a boat or a nest for a duck, complete with eggs.

Driftwood from the beach, drywood from the forest

(*Above*) Dried digitalis sprays provide an interesting setting for an unusual piece of twisted wood—which, incidentally, was purchased from a commercial source.

(*Opposite*) A dry branch festooned with Spanish moss dramatizes the smoothness of wood from the beach.

Keep it simple

An unusual object calls for a simple arrangement. This shape has great interest. Use a plain mat, a rock or two, and very little else.

Or make it dramatic

Rules are made to be broken. Here five objects of equal interest are combined to make one "main object"—a scene. There are two pieces of wood, a rock, an anise flower pod and a figure, with small pebbles added to balance the base.

Interest is more important than any set of rules

Artists and photographers have a time-honored rule which says that odd num-bers are better than even numbers for composition. They sometimes call this the "rule of three," using three objects of varying size to make quick and effective arrangements. This is a good rule which you can use to advantage in your own arrangements. This rule and others have been broken (opposite) with very happy results. Although the use of pairs can often lead to monotony, they have been used effectively here. There are two pieces of wood, two pine cones, two deer. The nine-inch teakwood base is interesting in itself. Actually, the base was used to raise the height of the arrangement as well as to provide a stage for the scene. And the discerning eye will discover the "rule of three" in the three levels of the arrangement; the higher pine cone, then the larger piece of wood upon which one deer is resting, then the lower cone and the smaller piece of wood upon which the other deer rests.

In arranging, the most important of all rules is found in the answer to the question, "Is it interesting?" If it is, you can forget all the rest.

Use mats wisely

The little figure above seems to be making a speech, so place him on a big stage. The background arrangement is secondary in importance.

The larger figure, opposite, dominates the scene. Add to his importance by using a raised platform, and keep the arrangement around his feet compact.

Four easy steps to an arrangement

Make your arrangement in four simple steps. Just as in flower arrangement you must choose your material, select a main object, give it a dominant position, balance it with secondary objects.

1. The driftwood seems to call for something on the right.

2. Still the arrangement doesn't balance; it seems to lean toward the left.

3. Add a third level of material. It fills out and supports the arrangement.

4. Rocks in the foreground make it complete.

Variety is spice

The use of contrasting materials adds greatly to the "flavor" of your arrangements. Notice the contrast in these arrangements between wood textures, rocks, thistles, seed pods. On the opposite page a colorful porcelain figure provides even greater variety

One piece of wood in three arrangements

A single piece of wood, with needle holder and clay holding it in the same position, can give you a variety of arrangements. Try your piece with other wood, with moss and seed pods, with a figure.

Give pieces like these plenty of space

Both pieces around which these arrangements have been built suggest sun and wind.

(*Above*) The pods are spread widely behind the rock, and the figure seems to look outward into space.

(*Opposite*) A similar effect has been achieved with an entirely different piece of wood. (This one, incidentally, was obtained from a commercial source.)

These arrangements imitate nature

Both pieces came from the Pacific Northwest. The one above might be standing in an open field, with horses seeking the shade.

(*Opposite*) This gaunt, blasted piece should stand high and alone. Our arrangement merely gives it a base—a lonely hilltop.

Strong lines need simple treatment

The strongest lines in art—and nature—are simple ones. The antique cypress tree root above, despite its interesting texture and twistings, is a strong and simple curve. It is quite in harmony with the modern black container, which also has a strong, simple line. Clay and rocks hold the wood in position.

(*Opposite*) The line is simple again—an ascending curve. With such a piece we use only a few weeds, also going upward.

In arrangements such as these, use as little material as possible. A few rocks at the base will often suffice.

Similar arrangements with different material

You can use many kinds of natural material to make your arrangments. Here are three vertical groups. A bit of twisted root, a hollow branch, or driftwood—they're all good. For your base use pebbles, burrs or just the wood itself.

This one can stand alone

Sometimes nature does your arranging for you. This piece was found on the beach at Carmel, California. The wood itself is an interesting combination of white and several shades of brown. Sun, wind, water, and wood-boring creatures have created a texture and shape which make it an arrangement in itself. All you need provide is a mat

A little pruning
sometimes helps

Gilded eucalyptus pods were used in this arrangement. They were not nearly as effective until the leaves were cut away.

Weeds and wood should harmonize

Since the branch above has a light thin feeling, the weeds are chosen to carry this out. Notice how the rocks at the base seem to balance this airy arrangement and give it a solid foundation.

(*Opposite*) Because the shape of this Oregon beach wood suggests a flowering plant, full blooming weeds are used. In this rather formal grouping, the weeds are arranged to repeat the form of the wood. Notice, though, that this is not an exact repetition; the tallest of the weeds gives an exaggerated feeling of height.

It can be as simple as this

A figure and a branch can make a whole arrangement. This figure is thirteen
inches high. The digitalis branches are held in place by a needle holder behind
the rocks. The figure is placed slightly to the right of center because he is
looking toward the left.

For instance: A placid pool

There's no water in this arrangement, but the feeling of water is everywhere in it. The wood, found by a river bed, suggested the arrangement. Johnson grass and gilded eucalyptus pods without leaves were set up to resemble the characteristic pool-side vegetation. A gleaming masonite mat became the pool. Two porcelain fish and a goose completed the picture.

This has the feeling of flowing water

Stones and wood like this seem to go together naturally. They might suggest the bank of a swift small stream, a tree undercut by water, and the stones worn smooth. Start with the wood. Tilt it. The slanted line gives it movement. **Let** the pebbles follow in this direction, flowing out from the base.

Stand them on end

Vertical arrangements are often good because they repeat the natural direction in which wood grows. In the arrangement above, only clay is used to hold the wood erect. These pieces came from Carmel, California.

(*Opposite*) This lumber-like piece of wood was found on the desert. Wind, sun and sand have given it a light polished finish. The split rocks with their flat planes have a feeling of desert and mesa country, and the inquisitive porcelain horse makes the scene complete. The wood is held on end by a needle holder and clay.

Use your material in many ways

Look at your material from all sides. Try it standing. Turn it around. Lay it down.

Here one piece of wood has made three strikingly different arrangements. With each change of position, a different group of secondary materials has been used. In one there are sharp rocks, artichoke blooms and weeds, in another smooth pebbles and lichen-covered branches, in the third a figure, anise and seed pods.

Your arrangement can change a figure

An amusing little figure like this can be just what you make him. Place him above the scene, looking down. You can almost hear his derisive cackle.

Let him peer out from below, and he becomes a very timid little goose.

Your precious wood: cut if you must

This piece is eighteen inches long but originally was much longer. It has been cut to make use of the most effective part. A simple plywood base has been nailed to the cut end, and in the arrangement a rock holds it firmly in place.

Colors added greatly to the harmony of this arrangement. The wood is a warm brown, the weeds are darker brown, the rocks are brown and white, and the horse is brown and white porcelain.

Be as original as you like

Give your imagination free play. You can make a complete scene or a simple abstraction. It can be dramatic, funny or serene. Do as you please and you'll please everyone.

Make it modern

The stark, simple lines of this piece of wood make it exceptionally good for a modern arrangement. The modern horse "fits," where another figure might have seemed out of place.

Make it traditional

The mass of this wood has dignity, the texture suggests age. The Chinese figure carries out the feeling of tradition and antiquity.

Let the wood suggest your style

The piece opposite has strong lines. It is clean and simple. The arrangement should be simple, too. The lichened wood, above, calls for something altogether different.

Don't be afraid to use oddities

This queer item is a piece of dried seaweed. It needs only a base to become a conversation piece. Because its form is so involved it would be most effective against a bare or very simple background.

Nature is full of the strange and the fantastic—good material for you. The light wood in the background might suggest a mountain, but the darker wood in the foreground, used for accent, is pure abstraction.

One piece makes three arrangements

You can have an endless variety of effects with only one main object. Change its surroundings. Add new material.

(*Above, left*) I used rattail statices, anise and a very small figure. (*Right*) I used capsia, dock and a figure. (*Opposite*) Here are silvered eucalyptus leaves and pods, and teasels.

These might be Hollywood sets

Sometimes your arrangements will become very real. The simplest materials will grow into complete landscapes.

Bits of bark, stones, seed pods and common weeds went into these.
One word of caution: Keep the arrangements *simple*. Don't try to crowd them with detail.

Have fun with figures

Two more representational, or landscape, arrangements. Here, action and interest are created by the groups of vari-colored horses.

In the scene on the opposite page, bare slab-like rocks and the single weed branch with its sparse seed pods are placed so that they give an arid, desert feeling.

When buying figures to use with your arrangements, look for those with movement or a natural pose.

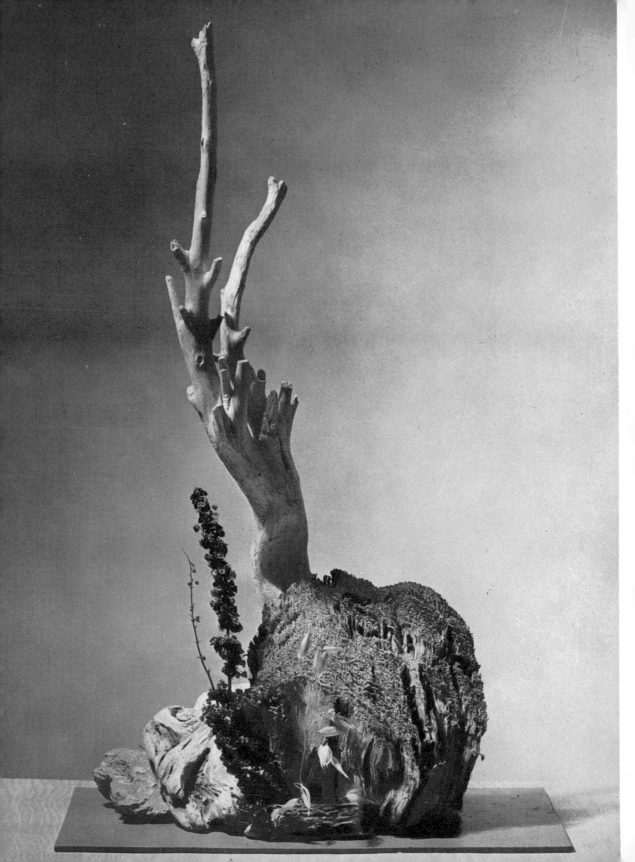

Textures in wood have great interest

Here are two arrangements which take full advantage of the interesting textures to be found in wood. These are both definite "landscapes," suggesting scenes in the mountains. In the arrangement below, notice the careful placement of the figure. Take him away or place him anywhere else and the unity of the arrangement would be lost.

Use strong material all by itself

Occasionally you'll want to use rocks, branches or driftwood so dramatic that they overpower everything else. Pieces like this have a strength of their own. Give them room—let them stand alone.

See your material from all sides

When you have selected a main object, study it. Look at it from above and below. Turn it around. See how the character changes with your viewpoint. A little time spent in studying your material will repay you many times in your arrangements.

These four photographs show four sides of a single piece of wood. Each could form the basis for a separate and entirely different arrangement.

Nature does it

Growth and erosion have developed these interesting shapes. With such objects, there's little for you to do. Give them a base—and enjoy them.

Choosing the base, however, is important. The shape and size of the mat should be in proportion to the shape and size of the object.

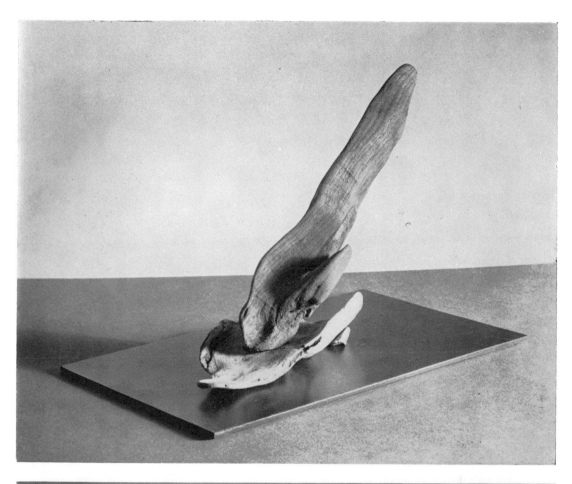

Sometimes wood looks like birds

Resemblances in nature are often startling. Use them. These are obviously a duck with eggs, and the great American eagle.

Notice how the material and texture of these pieces of wood accent the resemblance. The toughness, above, goes well with the eagle. The smoothness, opposite, suggests the old phrase "like water off a duck's back."

Fanciful or fantastic

Turn your imagination loose when you make arrangements. Be as whimsical as you like.

(*Above*) The design and texture of the light brown desert wood are interesting in themselves. When the little fawn was added the arrangement took on a fairy-tale quality.

(*Opposite*) These pieces of driftwood were bleached and polished on the sands at Carmel, California. They might be two animals, mother and child.

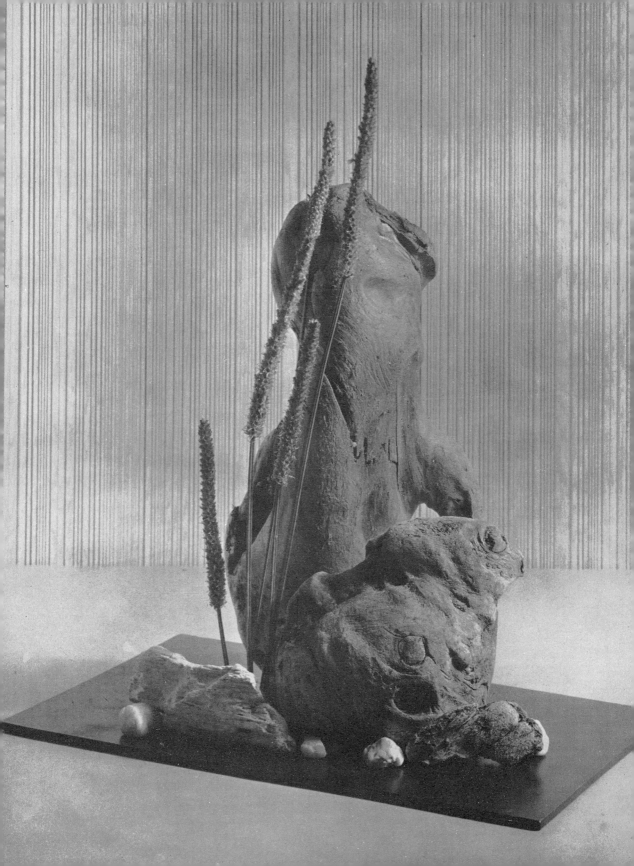

A peaceful grove

a prehistoric monster

(*Opposite*) Six slender stalks of wild oats become a grove of trees and dominate the scene. The bark here becomes simply a background. Rocks give the grove a solid base, and the figures give it the illusion of height. Actually the tallest of the oats is only thirteen inches high.

(*Above*) A long-billed prehistoric monster raises a sleepy head. Notice how the rocks at the left, although they do not touch it, seem to give support to the head.

Let your arrangements tell a story

This is one of the most imaginative kinds of arranging. Give your group a little plot. Let something be happening. The figure of the horse is poised, ready for action. The wood, eucalyptus leaves and pods point in the same direction.

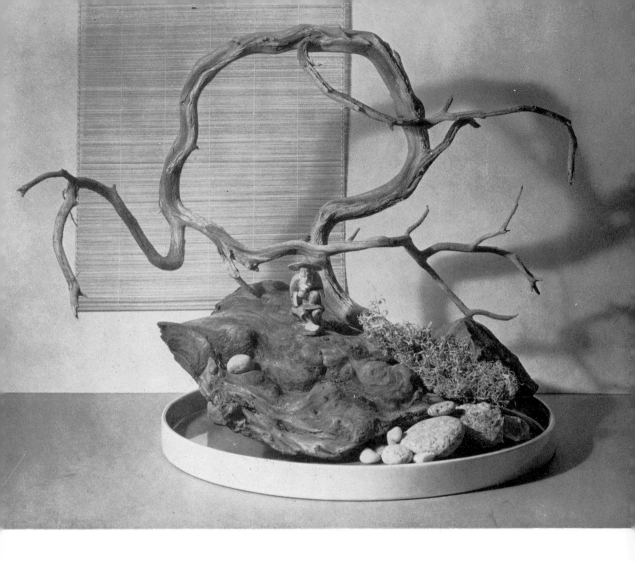

Here we have a philosopher, deep in thought. Twisted old roots and branches like these need a heavy base. Rocks in the foreground balance the height of the wood.

Use varied heights

The three levels of classical flower arrangement have been used with the sugar pine cones above. Actually, the two larger cones were almost the same height, so one was placed on a rock and anchored with modeling clay.

The arrangement opposite has three principal levels. First, the branch at the left. Then the group which includes the figure, the Johnson grass and cattails. Finally, and lowest, the wood and rocks in the foreground.

Smooth and rough — each has its charm

Two smooth stones repeat the form of this unusual piece of Oregon driftwood. (*Opposite*) Contrast in color and texture is used effectively. Both pieces are beach wood. The large dark background piece is barnacle-covered, while the porous gray foreground piece has been polished smooth.

Big or small

Your arrangement can be as large as a table or as small as your hand. Note the comparisons on these two pages.

Generally, two factors will determine the size of your arrangements: the material you use, and the location. If your arrangement is small, place it where it will be seen. If it is large, it is apt to need plenty of space around it.

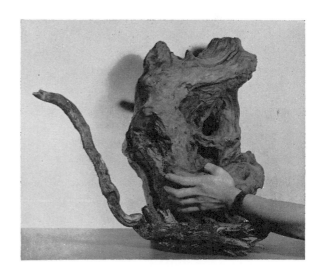

How to use unusual mats and stands

When your arrangement is very severe or simple, or when you wish to show a single piece, unusual mats and stands can add interest and importance.

The bamboo mat above has movable sections. They can be adjusted to balance the shape of your arrangement.

(*Opposite*) Any object gains in importance when you raise it up into the air. The teakwood stand makes this arrangement a museum piece.

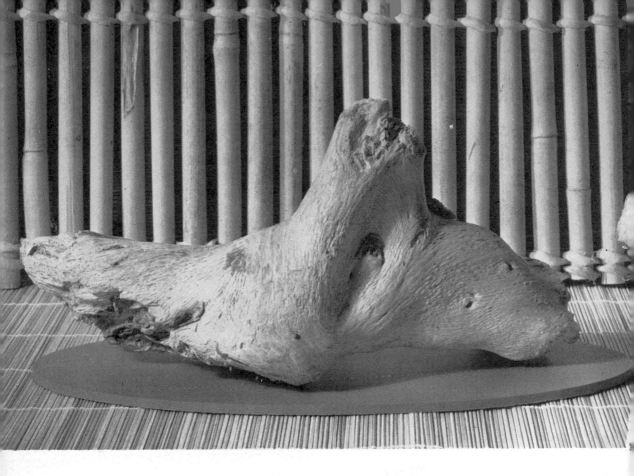

Give it an interesting background

Occasionally an unusual background will help an otherwise plain arrangement. Observe how the vertical lines of the bamboo mat offer a needed contrast here.

Use as much as you like

There are more than twenty individual pieces in this arrangement. These include five pieces of wood held in place by clay, plus miscellaneous rocks, seed pods and small figurines.

Stop before your arrangement begins to seem cluttered. But as long as it *helps* the total effect, use as much as you like.

Choose figures that fit the arrangement

Modern wood sculpture offers many excellent figures with clean simple lines, like that below. Such figures should be chosen with great care, however. The unusual form of the driftwood itself is almost enough here.

(*Opposite*) The delicate tracery of branches calls for a figure of intricate workmanship and great dignity. Foliage includes anise, digitalis, oats and lichen.

This can be used in many ways

When the shape is interesting, wood like this can be used again and again in combination with secondary materials. Let your imagination be your guide.

Dry cactus stalks

These strange pieces came from the desert. They are dry cactus stalks, held in place by clay and rocks. Purple cactus seed pods and branches of yellow anise add interest.

Repetition can add a lot

Just as the repetition of shapes and forms is used in painting and photographic composition, it can be used to produce effective arrangements.

(*Above*) The shape of the object is partially repeated in the mat. (*Opposite*) The background tray repeats the shape of the low container.

You can buy your material

Many department stores and florists carry leaves and branches which have been
spray-painted to preserve them. You can use them very effectively.
These are silvered eucalyptus leaves and pods.

All of the materials in this arrangement are silvered. They were purchased from a commercial florist and include eucalyptus leaves and pods, cattails and Johnson grass.

Such materials are also available in pink and violet tints and in gold. If you have access to spray-painting equipment you can even do your own tinting.

With leaves or without them

This arrangement is essentially one of leaves. The wood in the foreground is secondary and serves as a base. The leaves and pods are silvered eucalyptus, purchased from a florist.

A spray of silvered eucalyptus pods is the main object, with the other elements secondary in importance. When purchased, the spray was similar to those shown on the preceding pages. For this particular effect, the leaves were cut away.

One piece of bark in four arrangements

In these four arrangements, the main object is the same. It is a piece of bark nine and a half inches high. Found by a river, it appears to have been water-soaked, then tossed to the bank and bleached in the sun. Bits of dry moss are still embedded in it.

A variety of arrangements may be obtained by changing the secondary material. You can use rocks or wood for the base. Rattail or dock or wild oats provide incidental interest. If you use figures, they will influence the character of the arrangement. The porcelain horse gives it a modern feeling; the Chinese figure imparts a sense of antiquity.

In each of these four arrangements the bark remains in the same position and retains the major interest.

Let a figure give it size

Some of your arrangements will seem incomplete. They are good, but something is lacking.

Try adding a small figure—it will make your main object appear larger.

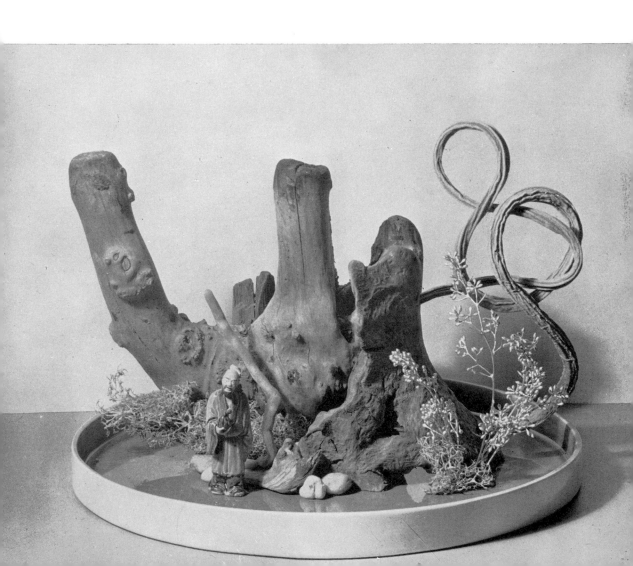

The figure sets the mood

Here are two arrangements which make use of fine modern wood sculptures.
With such material you can make a pool, with a water-nymph—or a tree, with
a wood-nymph.

Change the angle

This handsome piece of light gray driftwood came from Puget Sound. It is thirteen inches high. It was purchased from a commercial source, and one end had been cut off to make it stand upright without other support.

For our arrangement, however, the angle was wrong. The photographs show how the angle was changed without cutting the wood. All it required was a rock and a bit of clay.

FROM THE BACK

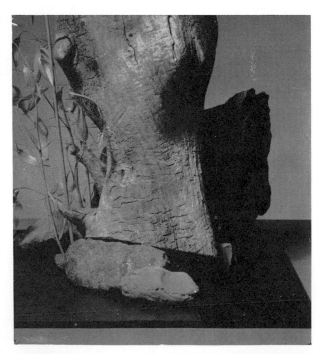

FROM THE FRONT

These are both from the desert

The pieces shown on these pages are both from the desert, but sharply different in form.

The bleak, slender branch above suggested a rather sparse arrangement. Seed pods, anise and a woven tray for background complete the group.

The massive piece, opposite, suggested age and the Orient. Again a Chinese figure was used, this time seated under a sprig of anise to represent an ancient plane tree.

Using unusual shapes

On the next four pages are arrangements which make use of very unusual shapes in very different ways.

The arch of the wood above suggests a natural bridge. This in turn suggests water. Notice how the nymph leaning against the bridge repeats the form of the erect bare branch behind her.

This knot, found on Carmel Beach, has great beauty and ample interest. It can stand by itself. Three rocks and a few sprigs of *immortels* help to place it and tie it down.

This piece could be used in many arrangements. Here it is part of a landscape.

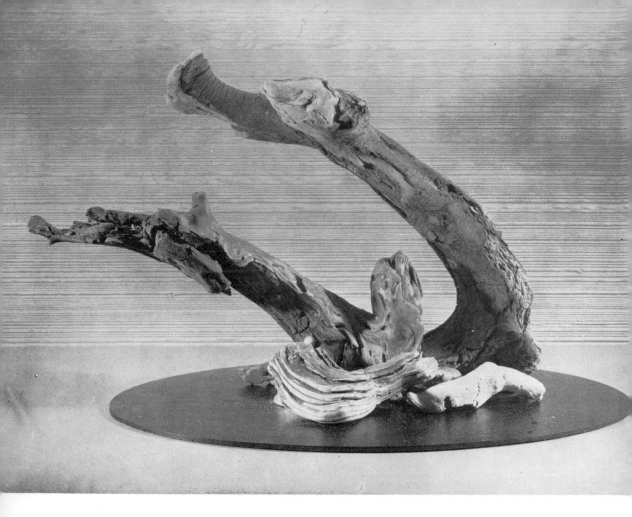

Here is a driftwood collector's dream. It has strong lines—it seems vaguely to suggest many things. This almost surrealist arrangement uses repetition most effectively. See how the two ends reach outward toward the left, in the same direction, with the same curve.

A piece like this has possibilities. Turn it around. Tip it up. Stand it on end.

In direct contrast to the piece on the opposite page, this one seems almost human, huddled inward, grotesque and terrified.

Again, as nearly always with such extraordinary specimens, the treatment is simple. A few pebbles, a few branches. The festooned lichen might be cobwebs—spectral, ghostly.

The answers to these three questions
will help your arrangements

The preceding pages have shown many types of arrangement, using many different types of material. Some have been direct and representational. Some have been abstract. Some have been traditional and others modern. There are as many different ways to arrange as there are different people in the world. Your own arrangements should reflect only yourself—your own personality, your own ideas.

But—where shall we start? Always, you start with a single object: a piece of driftwood, a figure, a branch, a stone. Whatever it is, this object will form the foundation upon which your arrangements are built. We have found it helpful to ask three questions about this object:

1. Where did it come from?

2. What does it suggest?

3. How shall we use it?

On the following pages several objects are examined, these three questions are answered, and an arrangement made. Perhaps you will find these questions helpful, too.

1. What did it come from?

   This piece of antique cypress tree root came from Carmel, California, where cypress continues to grow century after century despite storms, tides, and winter winds.

2. What does it suggest?

   The tremendous power of growing things to survive against all the forces of nature.

3. How shall we use it?

   With growing things—in this case cotoneaster, springing up like the eternal undergrowth.

1. Where did it come from?

    These are Sugar Pine cones from the Sierra Nevada region of California. More simply, they are from an evergreen forest.

2. What does it suggest?

    A forest scene.

3. How shall we use it?

    Directly, in a landscape, a forest scene. Trees, a fallen log, a deer, and we have an arrangement.

1. Where did it come from?
   This manzanita branch came from barren, rocky country.
2. What does it suggest?
   Perhaps a tree, swept by storms, blasted by lightning.
3. How shall we use it?
   In a bleak, barren, natural setting. Only bare rocks are added.

1. Where did it come from?
   This twisted piece of wood was found on the desert.
2. What does it suggest?
   Dry country.
3. How shall we use it?
   With flat rocks and thirsty horses—a landscape from the American desert.